Cou

C000160744

*L*og

South Downs - East
East Sussex

Publishing Ltd

www.countrysidedogwalks.co.uk

First published in October 2014 by **Wet Nose Publishing Ltd**,
Summer Roost
Graigfechan
Denbighshire
LL15 2EU
All enquiries regarding sales telephone: 01824 704398
email cdw@wetnosepublishing.co.uk
www.countrysidedogwalks.co.uk
ISBN 978-0-9573722-8-3

We would like to thank Daisy Gibbs

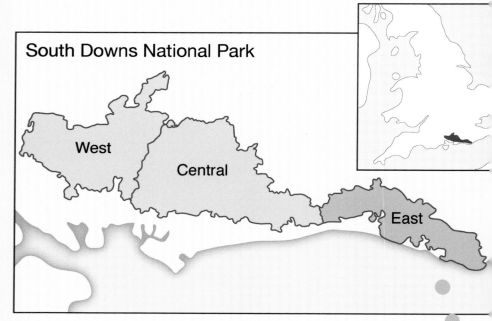

South Downs National Park

West

Central

East

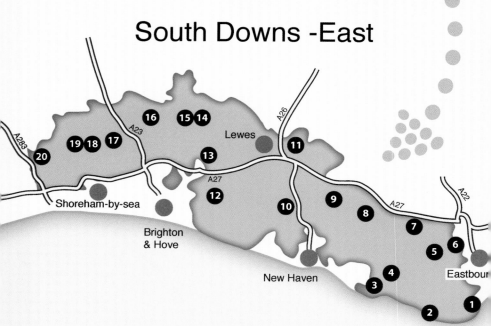

South Downs -East

A283

A23

16 15 14

Lewes

A26

19 18 17

11

20

Shoreham-by-sea

13

A27

12

10

9

8

A27

7

5   6

4

Eastbour

3

New Haven

2   1

Brighton
& Hove

A22

Contents

Introduction

The twenty walks included in this book are all designed so that you and your wet nosed friend have a really enjoyable time. Where there are stiles, they are specially designed with lift gates for dogs. At a quick glance there is information at the beginning of each walk to tell you what to expect and what you may need to take with you. The descriptive guides will also warn of any roads ahead or areas of livestock so that you can get your dog on the lead well in advance.

Dogs just love to explore new places. They really enjoy the new smells and carry themselves a little higher with the added excitement. Going to new places gets you and your dog out and about, meeting new people and their dogs. It is important to socialise dogs, as they will be more likely to act in a friendly manner towards other dogs as they gain confidence.

The stunning pictures in this book are just a taster of what you can see along the way. Many of the walks have fantastic views and scenery. Some of the walks are wooded, offering shade on those hot summer days.

The walks are graded Easy, Medium and Challenging. They are all around one to three hours long, depending on your and your dog's pace. You may start with the easy ones and work up to the

challenging walks depending on your and your dog's fitness. Different dog breeds and dog age must be taken into account when you decide which walks to do.

Different breeds of dog have different levels of fitness. For example, bulldogs can only do short walks whereas a border collie or a springer spaniel are extremely energetic and difficult to tire out. It is recommended that you do some research on the breed of dog that you own to get to know what sort of exercise that they require.

You may have a walk that you are happy doing with your dog every day, but this book will show you new areas to explore with a change of scenery and a chance to meet new people and their dogs. Dogs love new places to visit and you will see the change in them as they explore the new surroundings, taking in the new smells with delight. You will fulfil both your life and your dog's just by trying somewhere new.

Some of the walks include bridleways, so you may encounter horses and cyclists. It is important to put your dog on a lead if you see horses approach. It is always helpful to say hello to the riders as they near so that the horse realises that you are not a threat.

The South Downs National Park

The South Downs National Park was designated in April 2011. It covers 628 square miles from Winchester in the west to Eastbourne in the east. The area includes part of Hampshire and parts of East and West Sussex. Although newly recognised as a National Park, the fight for designation has been going on since the 1920s to protect the iconic landscape from threats such as development of industry and housing, ploughing up of the herb-rich chalk downland, which is important for many rare and specialist species, protection from deforestation of its vast and beautiful wooded hillsides, and destruction of heathlands. The latter supports all of our British reptiles, some of which are very rare. The South Downs Way (SDW) long distance path is 100 miles long and crosses the length of the National Park, following the chalk ridge through Sussex and part of Hampshire. Many of the circular walks in this book have included part of the SDW.

There are numerous quintessentially English villages throughout the National Park, with many thatched cottages. The unique flint and red brick buildings and walls and split rail fencing are authentic to the area and highlight exceptional craftsmanship, using locally sourced materials. The flint and chalk is visible in ploughed fields and can be seen clearly on eroded grassy paths. It is used to surface many footpaths throughout the National Park. The timber for the fencing is sourced from the many sweet chestnut coppiced woods.

Ground Nesting Birds

Watch out for vulnerable ground nesting birds during 1st of March until the end of July. Dogs that stray off the main paths may disturb birds and chicks, possibly killing them or breaking eggs. Species to look out for are Sky larks, Meadow pipits, Curlew, Red and Black grouse, Snipe and Pheasants.

Some if not all of these birds are declining in numbers, due partly to their vulnerability when nesting. Dogs are a threat to them, even if treading on them unintentionally. Some other threats are foxes, badgers, stoats, weasels, birds of prey and crows.

Please help to protect these birds during the nesting season by keeping your dog on the paths when walking in open areas such as grassland, moors, heathland and scrub.

Rivers

Some dogs love water and will think nothing of plunging into the river. With the extreme weather conditions over the last few years, a river that may be safe for your dog to swim in can change in a matter of hours to become a swollen torrent that could wash your dog away. Please be careful when near rivers if there have been heavy periods of rain or if they look swollen or fast flowing. It is best to put your dogs on the lead, until you have assessed the situation.

Livestock

If you find that you need to cross a field with cattle or horses and they seem interested in you or your dog it is recommended within the Countryside Code to let your dog off the lead. Never try to get between livestock and your dog. Your dog will get out of a situation a lot more easily with speed than you can. It is usually only cattle with young calves that are a threat, or young heifers or bullocks that tend to get a little inquisitive. They will usually stop when they get close to you or your dog.

Most horses will come over for a fuss but a small proportion do have a problem with dogs. They may see them as a threat and will act to defend the herd. Horses that are out with a rider are completely different as they are not defending the herd, and as long as you keep a safe distance there should not be a problem.

Sheep are not a danger to you, but your dog can be a danger to them. Where sheep are grazing it is vital that you have your dog on a lead or under very close control. You will know your dog, but if you are unsure it is better to play safe and keep your dog on a lead. It is important always to have your dog on a lead when around lambs. Lambs have a higher pitched bleat and can be the size of a cat, and your dog may act differently amongst them.

Ticks

If you have been walking in areas where sheep graze you should check your dog for ticks. They must be removed as soon as possible. It is best to use tick tweezers, which are specially designed to remove the head and leg parts of the tick. Ticks can carry diseases and the longer they remain latched on to your dog the more the chance of spreading infections.

Forests

The forest walks in this book are a changing landscape, which makes them unique and interesting. Descriptions may change with time, for instance a path may be described as being in the shade of the forest, but as this is a worked forest a section could be clear felled at any time. Another change over the years could be where a view is described across a previously felled area. This could then be planted up and trees grown blocking the views. Paths may change but this is less likely. On rare occasions the Forestry Commission may temporarily close paths due to forest works but again this is even less likely on a weekend. Any changes to the path networks that may occur after the date of print will be updated on our website.

Does your dog fetch a stick?

Most dogs love sticks and will pick them up without any encouragement from their owners. Vets and dog trainers recommend that you should not throw sticks for dogs. They can cause nasty injuries, sometimes fatal as the stick can pierce the throat, or rebound off the ground and cause harm to your dog.

Please clean up after your dog

Always be prepared, having dog bags with you at all times. Once you have cleaned up after your dog, please keep the bag, until you see a bin. If there are no bins provided, then take it away with you to a roadside bin. Dog bags that are discarded on the paths or in the bushes are unpleasant and unsightly and will not degrade.

1. Beachy Head

Medium - 2.8 miles - 1hr 30min

This is a coastal circular walk, with cliff edges in parts, where you can see the famous Beachy Head lighthouse and views over Eastbourne and across the sea. The route passes through floristic meadows, hawthorn and gorse scrub and you will reach the starting point for the South Downs Way long distance footpath. You can have the option of a detour to the sea front. Keep your dog on a lead when near to the cliff edges. There is sometimes grazing in the area, so check for livestock.

How to get there – From Brighton take the A27 and just as you approach Eastbourne follow the signs for Jevington on the A2270. Continue on the Jevington Road, passing through the village. On reaching a road junction turn left and continue on the A259. Turn right on reaching the sign for Beachy Head and Seafront. Take a right hand turn following the sign for Beachy Head Countryside Centre. A little further along the road you will find the main car park and centre on your right.

Grid Reference – TV 589957   **Postcode** –BN20 7YA

Parking – Pay and display

Facilities – There are toilets and a visitor centre in the car park and a dog-friendly café half way along.

You will need – Dog lead, dog bags, water for your dog

Countryside Dog Walks - South Downs, East Sussex

The Walk

❶ Cross the road, opposite to the toilet block. Pass a walled bench area and follow the tarmac path that descends in the direction of the sea, and soon after turn right on meeting another path. Look out for a path on your left, just before you reach the second seating area. Take this path, descending the steps, and then turn left. You will have lovely sea views and Eastbourne is straight ahead.

Continue on this path through scrubby areas. Ignore another path on your left and continue. There are rolling grassy banks on your right below, with many wild flowers in the spring and summer.

Pass another set of steps on your left, and continue straight ahead through hawthorn scrub, where you can enjoy some shade on hot days. Ignore a path on the right and continue ascending on the South Downs Way (SDW) long distance footpath, where you can enjoy the spectacular views once more.

Follow the worn grassy track across the common, staying close to the scrub on your right. Soon you will pass a way-marker for the SDW, and as you continue

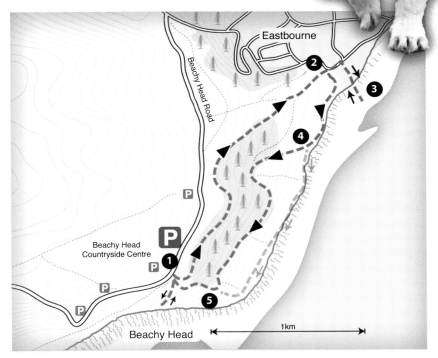

you will pass a way-marker signed for the Seafront. Follow the signs for the Seafront, passing between thick scrub.

You will leave the scrubby areas, where you continue to follow the sign for the seafront, descending towards Eastbourne, with views once more. As you near the road below, call your dog close or put him on a lead. ❷ Descend the steps, where you will see the interpretation panel indicating the start/finish of the South Downs Way long distance footpath. At this point you have the option of extending the walk for about half a mile to get access to the seafront, or just to the bottom of the hill, if you fancy some refreshments at the café below (option A). Option B is a shorter alternative.

A. For the seafront continue to descend to the bottom of the hill, otherwise skip this paragraph. Pass the dog-friendly café on your right. Continue straight ahead on the road, making use of the pavement. Take the first right-hand turn onto a private road beside Bede's School. Keep your dog on a lead as there is a cliff edge ahead. Continue to descend the many steps, where you will reach the pebble beach. ❸ Then simply retrace your steps back to the start/finish of the South Downs Way interpretation panel, and continue to option B below.

B. To skip the detour to the beach. On reaching the interpretation panel turn right to continue your walk (left if you are facing the panel). Put your dog on a lead as there is a cliff edge as you continue. You will ascend a hill and on reaching another path turn right. There are new views now as you are on the homeward stretch.

❹ There are two wide paths ahead - take the left path and descend. There are cliff edges ahead and a football pitch.

Pass beside the football pitch on your right and then you will have two options, a cliff edge walk (option A) or an inner path (option B). It is advisable if you choose the cliff edge to keep your dog on a lead.

A. Cliff Walk - When you reach the fork take the path on your left. The flowers are beautiful in the summer months, growing in the meadows across the hilly landscape. Continue on the short turf of the well-worn path. Descend a set of steps into a scrubby area.

On reaching another fork, you can take either path. The path on the right will take you across the middle of the meadow and a little further away from the cliff edge. Continue straight ahead, on the undulating path. Turn right to ascend the steep hill on reaching another path (or following the right bend

if you have continued with the cliff face). The path becomes quite steep. You will pass a post with a white top where the two routes combine. Keep your dog on a lead as the cliff edge is just beyond on your left.

B. Inner Walk – On reaching the fork, take the path on your right. Stay on the wider grassy path. On reaching another fork, take the right path, which ascends a little more steeply. On reaching another wide, stony path turn left. Providing there is no livestock in the area and you can keep him under close control, you can let your dog off the lead here.

Continue between the flower meadows on the undulating path. The sea and cliff edge are on your left and the scrub and hills are on your right. You will pass many benches along the route.

Where the path veers to the left, continue straight ahead on a minor path, ascending the steps on the steep bank.

A and B - Continue to a post with a white top where both routes re-join. **5** Put your dog on a lead here, as there is a cliff edge over on your left.

As you climb you will see two paths, one that veers to the right and a minor path, which continues to the top of the hill. Take the minor path.

On reaching another path at the top and a way-marker, turn left to reach a viewing platform, keeping dogs on a lead. If you look to your right you will see the well-known Beachy Head lighthouse. Turn back on the tarmac path, passing the way-marker once again, but now continue on the tarmac path, which will lead you back to your car. Remember there is a road ahead, so keep your dog under close control or on a lead.

2. Birling Gap

Easy - 1.5 miles - 1hr

This is a short walk close to a cliff edge, with stunning views to the beautiful Seven Sisters, which is a series of white cliff edges. You will pass a lighthouse and from there you will be able to see the famous Beachy Head lighthouse. There is also access to a wonderful flint and chalk pebble beach, beside white cliffs. Keep your dog on a lead whilst walking near to the cliff edge. Sheep graze at certain times of the year.

How to get there – From Brighton take the A27 and just as you approach Eastbourne follow the signs for Jevington on the A2270. Continue on the Jevington Road, passing through the village. On reaching a road junction turn left and continue through the village of East Dean. Take the second turn on your right, following the sign for Birling Gap. Continue to the end of the road, where you will see the National Trust car park.

Grid reference – TV 554960

Nearest Postcode – BN20 0AB

Parking – Birling Gap National Trust car park pay and display

Facilities – There is a Visitor Centre with toilets

You will need – Dog lead, dog bags, water for your dog

The Cliff Walk

❶ Keep your dog on a lead as there are grazing sheep and cliff edges. As you enter the car park from the road, head towards the building on the left. Take a path on your left, just before you pass the building. Ascend the steps and then look to your right for amazing views of the white cliffs known as The Seven Sisters.

Continue on the path, ignoring a path on your left. Continue on the well-trodden path, with the cliff edges a little further away on your right, heading toward the lighthouse. You will pass between scrubby areas, with coconut-scented gorse.

When you reach the lighthouse, go to the left of the lighthouse and pass around it. Cross over an access track and re-join the path ahead. You will see white cliff faces ahead, which are know as the Seven Sisters and a second lighthouse. This is the famous red and white Beachy Head lighthouse. This is the furthest point of your walk. **❷**

Birling Gap

Beachy Head Road

Belle Tout Lighthouse

1km

Turn around and after passing the lighthouse once again you can either re-trace your steps or take an inner path straight ahead, which will put a little distance between your dog and the cliff face if you prefer. ❸

If you have a good recall you can let your dog off the lead on the inner path. The hill has small pockets of heather. Cross the grassland area, veering to the right, until you reach a small ridge. Now follow the worn path. You will see the car park ahead and to your right.

Continue on the path, with the gorse scrub on your right. A little further along, cross a narrow path and continue straight ahead. On reaching a wider grassy path, turn right and descend to the far end of the car park.

The Beach Walk

This walk is not accessible during high tide. Care should be taken if walking some distance from the exit steps to ensure that the incoming tide doesn't trap you. Always check the tide timetable.

As you enter the car park from the road, head towards the building on your left. Pass the front of the building and continue, where you will see a platform with metal stairs (five flights).

Descend the stairs to reach the fantastic chalk and flint pebble beach, which is free from grazing animals so you can let your dog run free. The Seven Sisters look absolutely stunning from this point. ❹

Countryside Dog Walks - South Downs, East Sussex

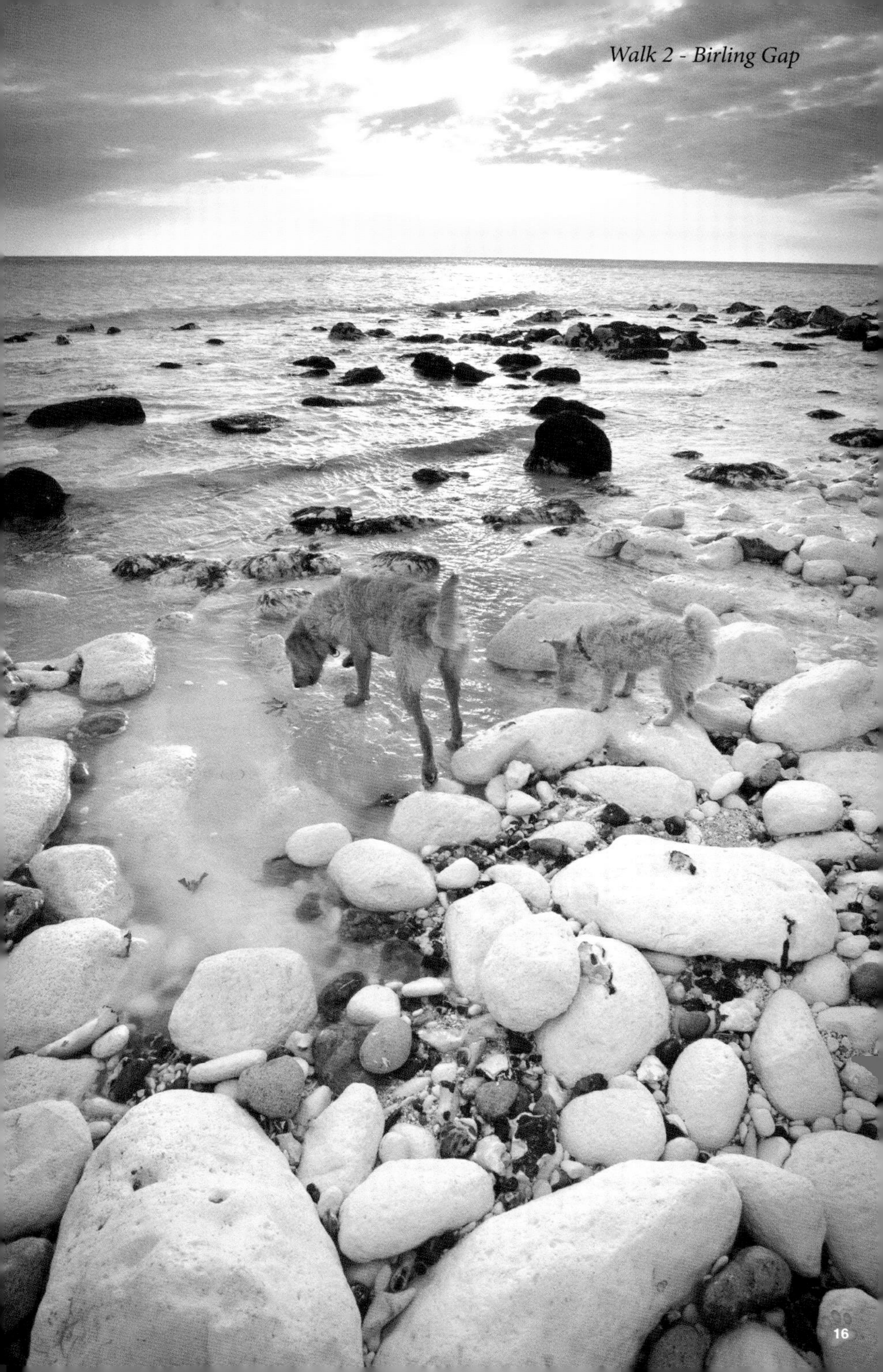

3. Seaford

Medium - 3.4 miles - 2hr

This is a beautiful estuary walk, passing through farmland, between hedgerows, and reaching a pebble beach where your dog can enjoy the tide. You will see the lovely white sea cliffs, known as the Seven Sisters. Pass through a lovely flood plain area on a raised path, where you can enjoy seeing many different types of wildfowl. There may be cattle and sheep grazing for parts of this walk. There is a road at the beginning and end.

How to get there – Take the A27, just outside Eastbourne heading in the direction of Brighton. Take the Alfriston turn-off and continue past Alfriston to Seaford. Follow the sign for Eastbourne on the A 259. Turn left, following the brown sign for Seaford Head Golf Course and Pool. Continue to the second mini roundabout and then turn left onto Arundel Road. At the end of the road turn left, onto Chyngton Road. At the roundabout continue straight on to enter Chyngton Way. At the end of the road turn right and continue to the car park.

Grid Reference – TV 503981   **Nearest Postcode** – BN25 4JB

Parking – Free in the car park

Facilities – There are no facilities

You will need – Dog lead, dog bags, and water for your dog

The Walk

1 From the car park entrance veer to the left and pass a building on your right. Pass beside a vehicle barrier to leave the car park. Take the middle path between the scrub. Cross a concrete track and continue straight on between the scrub and hedgerow.

You will see white cliff faces ahead known as the Seven Sisters. Pass through a gate on your right to avoid a cattle grid. There is a cliff edge on your right, so keep your dog on a lead or under close control. Ignore a stile on your left and continue beside the stock fence on your left, descending on the access track. You will pass through a kissing gate to avoid the cattle grid, and then pass some cottages on your right and descend to the pebble beach. You can stop here for a while and enjoy the sea air.

Continue along the sea front. There is a drop ahead, where the river enters the sea. **2** On reaching this, turn left, and follow up-stream of the river on your right. There may be sheep grazing this

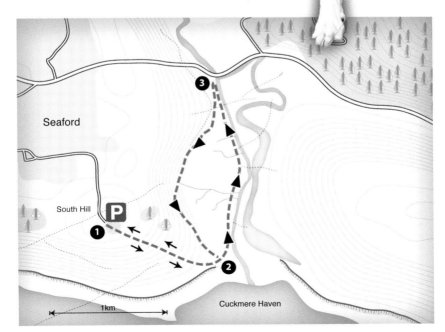

area. Pass through a gap in the fence and continue on the raised path between the flood plains. You may see wildfowl, herons and egrets here. The path veers away from the river, but there are ditches to your left.

Continue on this path, which bends sharply to your left, and you will soon see an interpretation panel. Go through the small gate on your left, just before reaching the interpretation panel. ❸ Keep your dog under close control as there may be livestock grazing.

Continue between hedgerows, with a ditch on your left, which is visible in places. You will pass a pond on your left and then the area opens up on your left. There may be cattle grazing in this area. Continue straight ahead, passing a track on your right.

You will see the white sea cliffs if you look to your left. Pass through a small gate ahead and continue straight ahead. Ignore a stile on your right. Pass trees and scrub on your left, which blocks the views for a short spell.

Pass through a kissing gate into a field with houses ahead. Continue close to the barbed wire fence on your left. You will now see the sea ahead. Descend to another kissing gate, and continue to the pebble beach once more. Take a familiar path on your right, passing the cottages once again. Remember, on passing through the kissing gate beside the cattle grid there is a cliff edge to your left. Continue on the access track and retrace your steps back to the car park.

4. Friston Forest

Easy - 1.6 miles - 1hr

This is a lovely circular walk through the forest. There is a little bit of ascent, but nothing too steep. Your dog will enjoy the freedom of running around as there are no roads and no livestock. You will have views of the White Horse in the distance as you make your way back down, on the edge of the forest.

How to get there - From Eastbourne take the A27 heading towards Brighton. Turn left at the cross roads, following the sign for Litlington and The Long Man. Pass through Wilmington Village, with views of the Long Man on your left. Pass through Litlington Village and after passing views on your right of The White Horse you will soon reach Friston car park on your left.

Grid Reference – TQ 517002

Parking – Pay and display in the car park

Facilities – There are toilets in the car park

You will need – Dog lead, dog bags and water for your dog.

The Walk

❶ At the furthest end of the car park veer right, passing the toilet block on your far right. Follow the sign for the White Horse View. Continue on a wide path, ignoring an immediate path on your left. Ascend on this path, ignoring paths on your left and right.

❷ On reaching another path turn right. After about fifty yards turn left and continue to ascend. There are colourful flowers lining the path in the summer months. You will pass a turning area for forest operations. The gradient lessens and then levels off altogether.

❸ Just as the path begins to ascend once again take the next path on your left. Follow the green way marker, ascending on a grassy path. The path then descends to a fence at the edge of the forest. Turn left, where you will see the White Horse on the hill in the distance ahead.

Continue on the edge of the forest with the stock fence, farmland and views on your right. You will pass a bench on your left, where you can stop for a while to enjoy the views. The path descends and you will cross another path, which is the South Downs Way long distance path. Continue straight ahead, entering back into the woods. **❹**

Ignore a path on your right and continue. The woods thicken and are mostly beech trees, making the area darker in the summer months. Ignore paths on your left and right and continue straight ahead, following the green way markers, where you will eventually return to the car park.

5. Jevington

Challenging - 2.6 miles - 2hr

This is a wonderful circular walk, which ascends gently through a sloped valley. You will cross through quiet, peaceful farmland, and pass between mature trees. On reaching the highest point of your walk, you will be rewarded with beautiful views. For most of your descent you will be between stock fencing, where your dog can enjoy some off-lead freedom. There is livestock for parts of this walk and a short section of quiet road.

How to get there –From Brighton take the A27 and just as you approach Eastbourne follow the signs for Jevington on the A2270. Continue on the Jevington Road, and pass to the other side of Jevington Village, where you will see the car park on your right.

Grid Reference – TQ 562012

Postcode – BN26 5QJ

Parking – Free in village car park

Facilities – There is a tea garden (dogs welcome)

You will need – Dog lead, dog bags and water for your dog

Countryside Dog Walks - South Downs, East Sussex

The Walk

❶ Keep your dog on a lead to begin with. From the car park go back onto the road and turn left. There are no pavements so walk on the right hand side of the road. Take the second road on the right, which is Willington Lane.

Continue to the end of the road, passing cottages on both sides. At the end of the road go through the gate **❷** and continue straight on, following the worn grassy path. Cross another less obvious track and continue straight ahead. The path will veer to your left before reaching the boundary hedgerow.

Pass between the hedgerow and scrub, and then pass through a gate. Continue on the worn path between the field boundaries, which are lined with trees. Pass through another gate and continue to follow beside the fence line, at the field edge.

Ignore a stile on your left and a footpath on your right. The fields have scattered trees and scrubby thickets. On reaching the end of the field, pass through a pedestrian gate, beside the farm gate, and continue walking beside the barbed fence on your left, at the edge of the field.

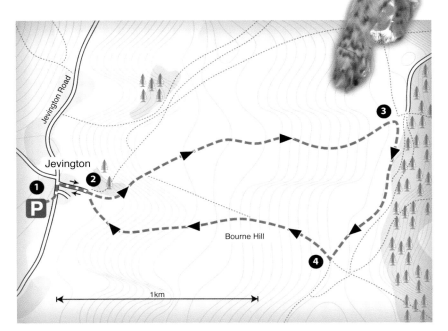

Ignore the stile on your left and continue straight ahead, once again to the end of the field. Pass through a gate, and walk between the trees and scrub on your left and the fence line to another field on your right.

The path ascends quite steeply. You can catch your breath and at the same time have a look behind at the views. Continue your ascent, and on reaching the top of the hill keep your dog under close control, pass through the gate and turn right. ❸ You will pass a car park on your left and on reaching a wide track turn right. You are now on the South Downs Way.

Looking to your right, you will have lovely views of the valley and the rolling hills, which meet at the bottom. On your left there is a grassy meadow, which gives wonderful colours in the summer months, attracting many butterflies and bees.

Ignore a path on your left and continue on the track, which begins to ascend gently. Another path joins the track; continue straight ahead, following beside the fence line.

❹ On meeting a junction of paths turn right, passing beside a vehicle barrier. The path now descends. Take the right path ahead, and if you look to your left on the horizon you can glimpse the sea.

You will have barbed wire fence on your right and scrub on your left and then a barbed wire fence. After a while you will be between hedgerows and the path becomes stony. Ignore a stile on your right. You will pass a sign warning cyclists to slow down. Call your dog close and put him on a lead, as you will be approaching a road.

Descend the quiet road, passing a tea garden on your right near the end. At the end of the road turn left onto another road and you will find the car park on your right a few paces along.

6. Willingdon

Easy - 2.6 miles - 1hr

This is an easy circular walk, which is popular for dog walking. You will follow part of the South Downs Way long distance trail. There are stunning views in all directions for much of this walk. You will continue beside floral meadows and scrub. There are many bees and butterflies in the summer months. At the furthest point of your walk you will reach a dew pond, where your dog can cool off. There are no roads on this walk but livestock may graze on the meadows for short periods.

How to get there –On the A27, just outside Eastbourne, take the Polegate/ Willingdon turn off (A2270). Continue through Willingdon and take a right turn onto Cooper's Hill, following the sign for Willingdon Village and Parish Church. Turn right again onto Butt's Lane. At the end of this road you will reach the car park.

Grid Reference – TQ 579017
Nearest Postcode – BN20 9HQ

Parking – Pay and display in the car park

Facilities – There are no facilities

You will need – Dog leads, dog bags

The Walk

❶ At the entrance to the car park, turn right and go to the end of the first parking bay. Turn left to join the South Downs Way long distance footpath, where you will have views on your right across the fields to rolling hilly countryside. There are floristic meadows on your left with some scrubby areas.

Continue straight ahead, on a path which is deeply rutted to begin with. There is a field boundary on your right. After a while the path ascends slightly and another path on your left merges with the path which you are on. Ignore a wide grassy path on your left. You will ascend and another path joins the path which you are on from your left, just before you reach the top of the hill. When you reach another track turn left, where you will see an old milestone signed Willingdon, Old Town and Eastbourne.

❷ As you turn a bend you will pass a gate on your right and a trig point on your left. You can see Eastbourne and the sea on a clear day. The meadows are beautiful in the summer months, attracting many butterflies and bees. On reaching a fork keep to the right, following the fence line.

Continue on the undulating path, passing amongst hawthorn scrub. The path descends. On reaching a dip in the hill, ignore the stile on your right

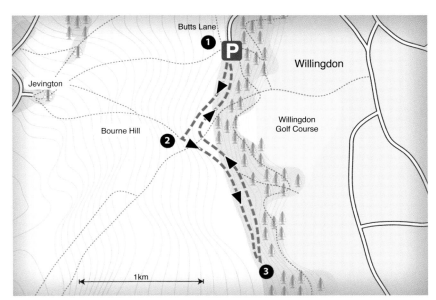

between the two farm gates and take a path on your left. Then cross another grassy track and veer right, heading towards a large concrete block.

❸ You will reach a dew pond where your dog can cool off. This is the furthest point of your walk. Turn around and continue on the path ahead, ascending amongst hawthorn scrub. Continue on the path between the grassy meadows and a little further along you will be between gorse patches.

You will reach an open area once again. Continue on the path, which is parallel to the path which you walked on earlier. On reaching a fork take the path on your left, staying parallel with the outward path.

You will have views once again here. The path ascends and you will pass a path on your right. On reaching a fork near to the trig point on your far left, take the path on your right, which soon descends. Another path joins from your right. Continue straight ahead on a middle path, where several paths meet as you enter another scrubby area. Pass an aerial mast on your left and then a small woodland copse on your right, where you then descend back to the car park.

7. The Long Man

Medium - 2.2 miles - 1.5hr

This walk is partly linear and has a circular section at the furthest point. There is an ascent but it is gradual. You will pass through farmland on well-made tracks to reach the wonderful carving in the grassland, 'The Long Man'. You then have a circular walk around Wilmington Hill where you will see an ancient burial mound. There are wonderful views in all directions. There may be livestock grazing for most of this walk, but there are no roads.

How to get there – From Eastbourne take the A27 heading towards Brighton. Turn left at the cross roads, following the sign for Litlington and The Long Man. Pass through Wilmington Village, where you will find the car park on your right.

Grid Reference – TQ 543041
Postcode – BN26 5SW

Parking – Free in the car park

Facilities – There are no facilities.

You will need – Dog lead, dog bags and water for your dog

Countryside Dog Walks - South Downs, East Sussex

The Walk

❶ From the car park go back onto the road, passing the split rail fencing. On reaching the road, cross over and ascend the steps. Walk towards the Long Man in the distance, on a well-worn path between hedgerows, with hilly farmland on your left and ahead.

Pass around a wooden barrier and turn left. Stay on the well-worn path between the arable fields, keeping your dog under close control. As the path begins to ascend you will be between hedgerows. Pass through a gate a little further along, keeping your dog under close control or on a lead as there may be livestock grazing, possibly sheep and cattle.

Follow on the path straight ahead, ascending to a barbed fence just below the Long Man. **❷** Turn right on the path where you will pass an ancient burial mound on your right.

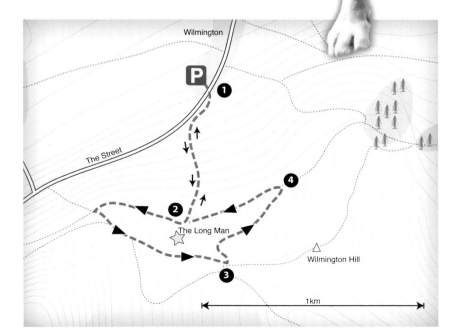

The views on your right are fantastic, with endless open countryside. Ascend the worn path, and a little further on, pass through a gate and turn left.

Ascend between two small hills, which have lovely wild flowers in the summer months. Join a sunken path when you see it veering to the right ahead. This is part of the South Downs Way long distance route. As you climb you will have views once again on your right.

Pass between the gorse scrub. The path will veer to the left a little further along, as you cross over the top of Windover Hill. You will pass another burial mound on your far left. Continue over the top of the hill, with views now on both sides.

Pass through a gate on reaching the stock fence and take the immediate left path at the fork, leaving the South Downs Way. ❸ Go through the gate on the left, just after passing the farm gate. Turn slightly left descending the hill, following the worn path, which is grassy to begin with and then chalk.

Pass the many small hillocks, and as the path bends to the right the gradient lessens. The path is now grassy again, and on reaching another path turn left, ❹ where you will see the Long Man once more. Continue on the path and on reaching a fork take the lower path. You will soon reach a familiar path. Pass through the gate on your right and retrace your steps back to the car park.

8. Bopeep

Med-Chall - 3.7 miles - 2.5hr

This circular walk follows the South Downs Way to begin with. It descends with wonderful views over rolling hills and extensive, patchwork-effect views across the countryside. You will pass through quiet farm tracks through the middle of arable fields. There may be livestock and there is a steep section of quiet road at the end of the walk.

How to get there – Take the A27 from Eastbourne heading in the direction of Brighton. Pass the turn-off for Alciston and turn left at the next cross roads, onto Bopeep Lane. Continue to the end of the lane, where you will reach the car park.

Grid Reference – TQ 494050
Nearest Postcode – BN26 6UJ

Parking – Free in the car park

Facilities – There are no facilities

You will need – Dog lead, dog bags, and water for your dog

The Walk

❶ There may be sheep or cattle grazing, so you will need to keep your dog under close control or on a lead. Go to the furthest end of the car park, away from the entrance, and pass through the gate onto a track and turn left. Pass through another gate and follow the track, where you are now on part of the South Downs Way (SDW) long distance footpath.

There are sea views on your right and extensive views on your left over countryside, with patchwork fields and villages. The path ascends gradually, across a field close to the edge.

You will pass a burial mound on your left and then a large depression. When the path bends sharply to the right, continue straight ahead, passing a finger post following the sign for the SDW. You now have a barbed fence line on your right.

Pass through a gate and turn left, now with a stock fence on your left. **❷** Look out for another gate on your left. Go through the gate, walking between

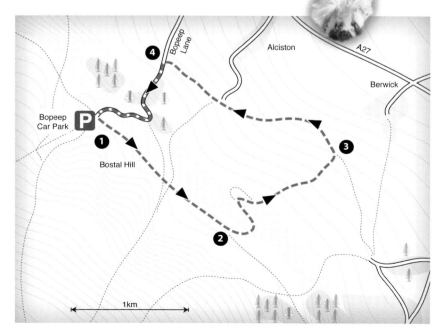

fields with stock fence on both sides. This is a bridleway so you may come across horses. Cross a track and descend along the path on the opposite side. You will now find that you are back on an open hillside, with views once more.

The path bends sharply to the left and cuts across the hillside. There are lovely rolling hills ahead. Pass through a gate and continue your descent. Follow the sharp bend to the right, staying on the main path. Cross the field descending to the level ground ahead.

Continue on the track between the hill and the hedgerow. Look out for a path on the right and ahead, marked with a blue arrow. Take this path, which follows the edge of the field, with the hillside on your right.

Pass through scrub, and then go through the gate and continue on the narrow path, between scrub, with fields either side. At the end of the path turn left onto a farm track. ❸ Keep your dogs under close control, as there may be farm vehicles or horse riders. You will pass a brick barn/house on your left. Continue on the track between two large arable fields.

Continue on the track, passing between another two large arable fields. The track will ascend, between hedgerows. Just after passing field entrances on your left and right you will cross another track, and continue straight ahead. The track will ascend once again, for a short section. Pass between the hedgerows, where you will need to put your dog on a lead, as you will pass through a private driveway.

Pass the house and on reaching the quiet road, turn left. ❹ The road ascends and is tree lined. Continue on this road, which is quite steep in places, where you will eventually reach the car park on your left.

9. Firle Beacon

Med-Chall - 4.5 miles - 2hr 30mins

This is a delightful circular walk, starting on the South Downs Way long distance footpath. The views are truly stunning on a clear day, where you will see across the rolling hillside to the extensive flat plains below. You can also have sea views for a short section of the walk. Returning along farm tracks, you will pass a dog-friendly tea garden 'The Beanstalk'. Then ascend back along the edge of arable fields and then through mixed broadleaved woodland. There may be sheep and cattle grazing for parts of the walk. Some of the tracks are also bridleways, therefore you may encounter horses or cyclists.

How to get there – From Brighton take the A27, heading towards Eastbourne. Take a right turn signed for Firle. Take the second turn on your right onto Firle Bostal, following the sign for Firle Beacon. Follow the winding road until you see the car park on your left.

Grid Reference – TQ 468059

Parking – Free in the car park

Facilities – There is a tea garden half way around the walk.

You will need – Dog lead, dog bags, water for your dog on hot days.

The Walk

1 From the car park take the gate on the left, near to the far end of the car park, just as it narrows. Follow the South Downs Way (SDW) long distance footpath, heading towards the corner of the fence line. You will have stunning views on your left across beautiful miles of flat landscape. This view will continue for much of the walk.

On reaching a corner post you should now follow close to the stock fence on your right. You will have sea views on your right. Pass through a gateway and continue straight ahead. Ascend to a gate where on your left you can see Firle Tower. Continue on the worn path.

You will pass a burial mound on your left and then a trig point. The path descends and you will pass another burial mound on your left. Continue for some distance and as you pass a gate on your right you will see a post on your left. **2** Take the path over on your left, indicated by the post, and descend the hidden grassy track across the hillside.

You will reach a stock fence on your right. Descend to the gate and then pass through it. Continue straight ahead on the wide sunken grassy path, with beautiful views on

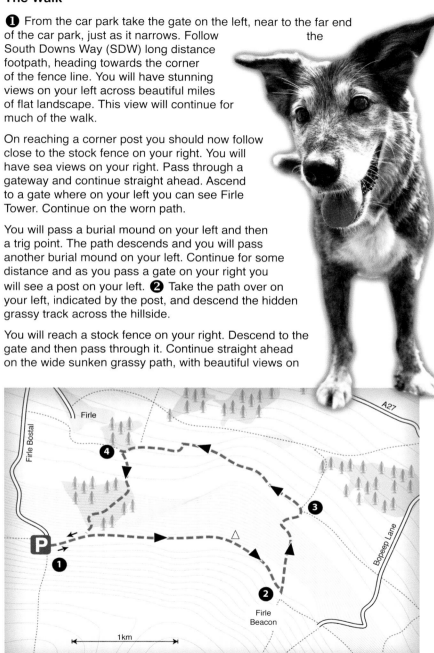

your right and ahead. At the bottom of the hill you will pass through a gate (before going through the gate there is a water feeder on your left, where your dog can get a drink).

Descend a wooded lane and on reaching the end turn left. ❸ Follow the wide farm track, which is tree-lined on your left, and there is a hedgerow on your right. The tree line ends at the top of the hill. You then descend at the edge of the arable field, where you can see Firle Tower ahead. As you continue there are hedgerows on both sides of the track.

At the end of the track you will reach Beanstalk Tea gardens. You can stop here if you wish to have refreshments. Turn left and continue on the track, which is now tree-lined. Pass some impressive mature beech and horse chestnut trees. Pass a lane on your right and ascend for a short distance.

As you reach a wall on your right at the top of the hill, take a path on your left. ❹ Pass through a gate (usually open) and continue on the track on the right of the field. Take the next path on your right, pass through a gate and take the first left hand path, ascending gradually through the trees.

On meeting another path turn right. Continue through the mixed broadleaved woodland - the path will steepen a little further along. At the end of the woodland, pass through a gate, and continue on the sunken path as you near the top of the hill. You now turn right on reaching a familiar path and retrace your steps back to the car park.

10. Southease

Medium - 3miles - 1hr 30min

On this circular walk your dog will be able to enjoy a splash in the River Ouse, providing the water is calm. You will follow this for part of the walk. In the summer months there are many colourful flowers that grow along the bund beside the river. You will pass through the quiet village of Rodmell, and then continue alongside peaceful arable fields. There is a gradual ascent, and you will then return to the village of Southease. There are some quiet roads, and at times there may be livestock grazing along the river.

How to get there – From Lewes follow the directions to Kingston. Pass over the A27 and continue past the turn-off to Kingston. Pass through Iford and continue on Piddlinghoe Road. On reaching Southease take the first turning on your left. Continue until you will reach a weak bridge. Parking is just beyond the weak bridge in a lay-by on your left, or alternatively before it on the grass verge. If you use satnav the postcode will bring you as far as the church. Continue past the church without turning off and follow the road straight ahead.

Grid Reference – TQ 427053   **Nearest Postcode** – BN7 3HX

Parking – Free in the lay-by

Facilities – There are no facilities

You will need – Dog leads, dog bags and water for your dog (river is saline).

The Walk

❶ From the car park bay, continue straight ahead to cross the road bridge. Ignore the footpath on your left, and shortly after take the footpath on your right. Continue on the well-made path. Pass through another small gate. Continue straight ahead, staying on top of the bund. There is another path, which is parallel on your left, below.

Pass through a gate and continue beside the river Ouse, which is tidal on your right. There is open pasture on your left, beyond the path. There are views ahead and to your right. In the summer months you will hear the chatter of warblers in the reeds on your left beyond the parallel path.

Pass through another gate and continue walking along the bund. There are meadow flowers in the summer months, which grow on both sides of the bund, adding colour to your walk. As you continue the views expand, with chalk hills ahead.

Pass through a kissing gate and follow the way-marker for the Sussex Ouse Valley Way. **❷** You will see a finger post on the lower path. Descend to the lower path, face the direction you have been walking in and take the path on your left, now walking away from the river. Continue on a track between meadows, with beautiful views ahead.

Pass through a small gate straight ahead and continue on the track, with a ditch on your left. You will pass through another gate and continue on the track. You will then see a church ahead and to your left. Put your dog on a

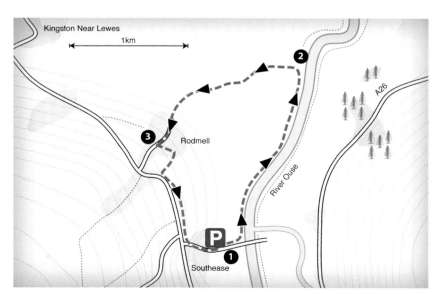

lead and go through a gate, where you will pass a water-treatment works on your left. Soon afterwards you will pass a livery stud on your right.

Trees now line the track on both sides. You will pass a car park on your left as you reach Rodmell village. On reaching a road, turn left and ascend a little way through the village, passing lovely flint and brick cottages on your right. Immediately after passing the National Trust Monk's House on your left, take the footpath on your left, which is signed for the School. ❸

Continue between the flint stone walls, passing the school on your left, and enter the church grave yard straight ahead. Continue beside the boundary wall on your right, not on the main path to the church. You will reach a stone stile - cross this and continue to a track, and turn right. Take the path on your right soon after. Continue between the split rail fencing, with houses on your right and gardens and allotments on your left. Pass some houses on your left and continue on the access track, between fields. Ascend the track, with a hedgerow on your right. Keep your dog on a lead, as there is a busy main road ahead.

Just before reaching the road, take the footpath on your left, which is signed for Southease. Keep your dog on a lead, as the footpath continues parallel with the road. The path starts off stony but then as you merge with a wider path it will be grassy. You will have rolling hills beyond an arable field on your left and a thick tree line on your right. On reaching a gate, pass through it and continue on the path, now with the hillside directly on your left. As the path bends sharply to your left, ascend the hill with some steps. On reaching the top of the steps have a look at the wonderful views on your left.

As you continue the path descends and veers away from the road. Pass through a gate straight ahead, descend the steps and turn right. You will now enter Southease Village. On reaching the quiet road turn left. Descend through the village, passing a lovely flint stone church. Ignore the road on your right (but if you do turn right, you will find a water tap and dog bowl beside the church boundary wall). Pass the village green on your right and continue on the road, which eventually crosses the bridge to your car.

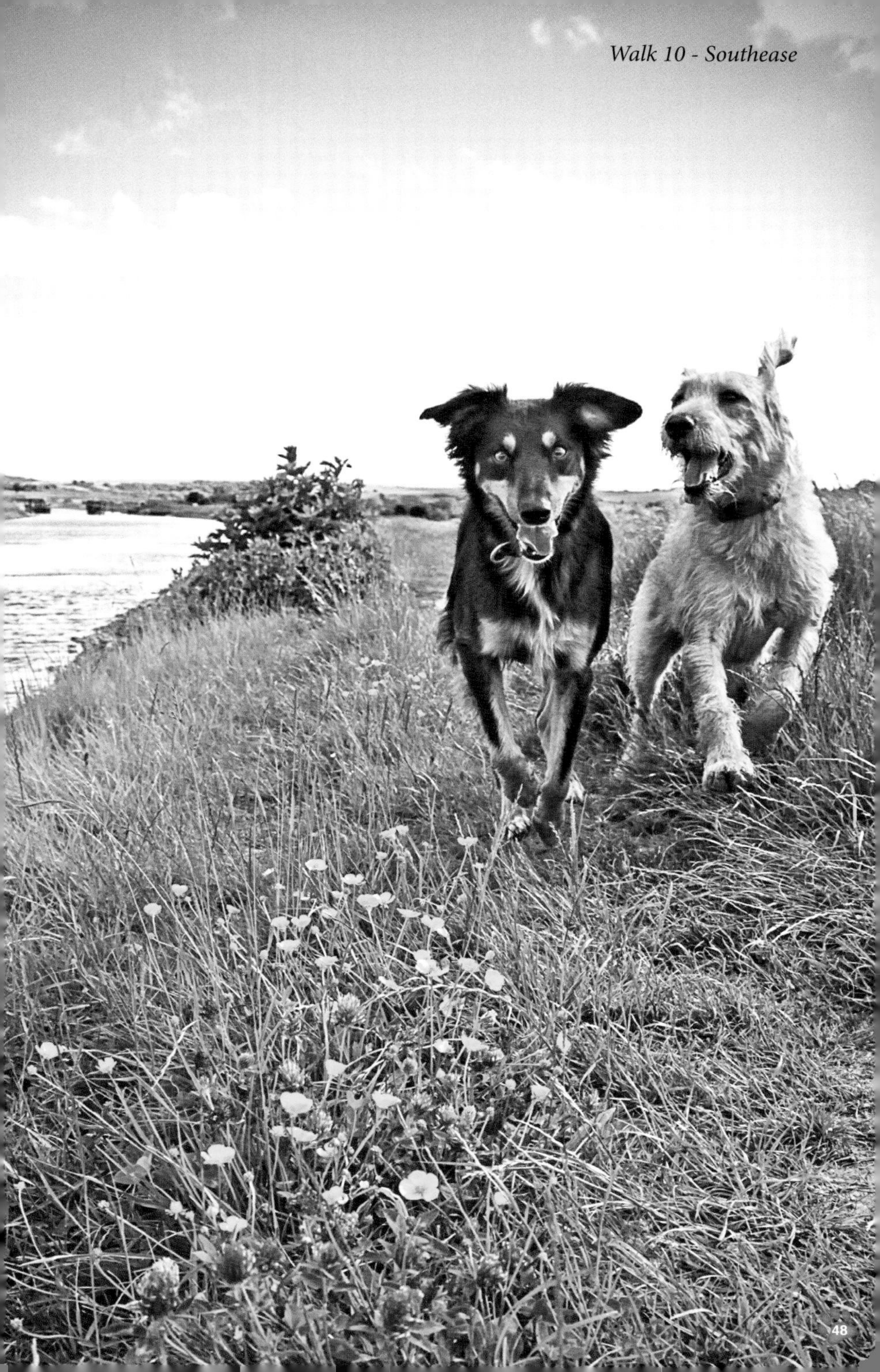

11. Malling Down

Medium - 1.8 miles - 1hr

This is a wonderful circular walk. A large section of the walk is within the Malling Down Nature Reserve, which is a disused limestone quarry. Now it is an unusual site, with many little hills and mounds, looking like a scene from The Hobbit! There is a small hill walk across Malling Hill, which is floristic in the summer months. Here you will have amazing views across Lewes and beyond. There is a mixture of woods and open hills and scrub on this walk. There may be cattle grazing, but there are no roads.

How to get there – From Lewes take the A26 heading towards Uckfield and London. Turn right on reaching the B2192, signed for Ringmer. A little further along the road you will find parking in a lay-by on the right hand side.

Grid Reference – TQ 433115

Parking – Free in the lay-by

Facilities – There are no facilities

You will need – Dog leads, dog bags and water for your dog

The Walk

❶ From the lay-by, face the road and turn left. Take the footpath at the end of the lay-by. Ascend and pass through a kissing gate into a Wildlife Trust reserve. Take the path, which veers away from the road. On reaching an interpretation panel continue straight ahead, ignoring the path on your left.

Pass between the scrub and continue straight ahead as you pass an opening, with views on your left into the disused quarry. Ascend gently between the banks, with scrub and trees on both sides. There are views on your left where the trees allow, looking across miles of countryside.

Take a path on your right, which descends into a woodland strip (roughly 50 yards before a gate on your left). Continue on a level path, which cuts across the wooded slope. At the end of the path pass through a gate and continue on a surfaced path between the trees.

The path descends gently and you will pass a disused quarry entrance on your left. **❷** Take the next track on your left, which ascends between the trees. You will reach a gate and two kissing gates. Go through the kissing gate, which is next to the farm gate straight ahead. There may be cattle grazing here.

Continue on the track. You will soon ascend between banks. As you ascend, there are views on your right across Lewes to the hills beyond. The track

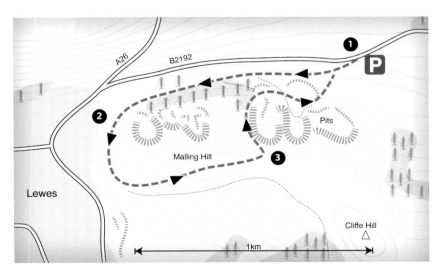

curves left. Continue through the middle of the sloped field. You will reach a small gate; pass through it and then pass through another gate, which is on your left a few yards ahead. There may be cattle in the field.

Follow on the slightly worn grassy path, horizontally across the field. You will soon see a mound ahead on your left, and there is also a golf course ahead to your right. On reaching the mound, keep it on your left and continue on the path. You will soon reach a gate. ❸ Pass through the gate, keeping your dog under close control as there is a cliff face on your right.

Turn left and continue on the worn path, with a fence line on your left and fantastic views on your right and ahead. There is a steep slope on your right, which is part of a disused quarry, and some fantastic hillocks below on your right, which were the remains of quarry waste. Nature has reclaimed the land and it is now grassed over with some scrub and wild flowers.

As you turn a bend, the path descends and there is an overgrown hedgerow on your left. Ignore a gate on your left and continue to descend between the trees. You will soon be on the opposite side of the quarry. The path becomes a little tricky, as it steepens with some loose stone.

On reaching another path, continue straight ahead on the narrow path between the banks. The path splits in two, and you should take the higher path on your right. Continue on the slope beside the hills (straight out of The Hobbit!) on your right. The path soon veers to your left and you will descend to reach a gate.

Go through the gate and turn right. There may be cattle here. Continue beside the fence on your right. When you reach another gate in the fence line, pass through it. Take the path on your left. Cross another path and continue straight ahead. The path soon veers left towards the fence line once again. Continue along the fence line and pass through another small gate, near to the corner of the fence.

Continue straight ahead, and descend on the wide path through the middle of the field, with views ahead. As you reach a sunken path, turn right. Descend between the banks, passing between the scrub. You will reach a familiar interpretation panel. Pass this and continue to the gate, where you will reach the lay-by.

12. Brighton Edge

Chall - 5.5 miles - 2hr 30min

This walk is literally on the edge of Brighton, and yet you could be forgiven for thinking you were miles from anywhere. After walking for a while along the South Downs Way long distance path you will have views across Brighton and beyond. A little further along you will be looking across Lewes and far beyond at the beautiful hilly landscape. You will then descend into a valley and cross some quiet agricultural fields. On your ascent you will pass through Castle Hill Nature Reserve, which is protected because of the chalk downs, which may be bursting with colour in the spring and summer. There may be cattle and sheep throughout this walk. Keep your dog on the paths during nesting season, as there may be ground-nesting birds such as skylarks. There are no roads.

How to get there – From the A27 take the Falmer B2123 turn off, just outside Brighton. Continue through Falmer heading towards Woodingdean, staying on the B2123. The car park will be found on your left hand side, just before reaching Woodingdean.

Grid Reference – TQ 356063   **Postcode** – BN2 6NT

Parking – Free

Facilities – There are no facilities

You will need – Dog lead, dog bags and water for your dog

Countryside Dog Walks - South Downs, East Sussex

The Walk

❶ Keep your dog on a lead at the beginning of this walk. From the car park go back to the entrance and turn right, and then immediately right again. Follow the track beside the car park. Take the path ahead and to your left, and pass around the vehicle barrier. You are now on part of the South Downs Way (SDW) long distance footpath.

Ascend gradually between fields towards the aerial mast ahead. There are views on your left across the countryside. On reaching the mast, keep your dog on a lead or under close control and pass through the gate, where there may be sheep grazing in the field. Continue on the worn track. The views will expand as you continue.

The path will descend a little. Ignore a gate on your right into Castle Hill and continue. On reaching a gate straight ahead, pass through it and continue on the track with a stock fence on your right. The path will now ascend on the edge of a field. There are sloping hills on your left.

As the path levels, your views extend and you will see the town of Lewes straight ahead. Continue with the fence line, where the paths split into two.

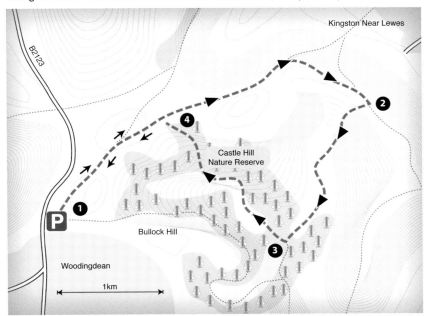

The path descends and veers away from the fence. Pass between gorse scrub, and a dew pond on your right.

On reaching a gate, go through it and continue on the worn path. Pass another dew pond on your right. You will pass a ring of split rail fence on your left, with a dew pond within. Continue straight on with views on your left. Pass a finger post on your left and continue straight ahead.

Pass through a small gate and continue to follow on the worn grassy path. On reaching a gravel track turn right. ❷ Go through the gate beside the cattle grid. Descend on the track between fences and fields as you make your way into the valley.

You will continue over a concrete track, passing a barn on your right. Pass through the kissing gate - there may be cows, so keep your dog under close control - and continue through the middle of a field in the bottom of the valley. On reaching the end of the field pass through the gate, and continue straight ahead on the worn grassy path through the middle of another field. Pass through a gate and again continue through the middle of a field.

Continue to pass through another gate and descend to reach close to agricultural buildings. ❸ Turn right on the track and ascend towards the trees on your right. Pass through a gate straight ahead, keeping your dog under close control or on a lead. Continue on the edge of a field with a grassy bank on your right. The path continues around two sides of the field. You will then begin to ascend, just before you pass through a gate.

Pass through the gate into Castle Hill National Nature Reserve. Ignore the paths on your left and right and continue straight ahead. Ascend gradually between the sloped, flower-rich meadows. The path becomes quite steep as you continue towards and amongst the hawthorn.

On reaching a gate pass through it and turn left. ❹ You are now on a familiar path. Retrace your steps back to the car park.

13. Stanmer Park

Medium - 4.3 miles - 2hr

This circular walk is brilliant for your dog. The woods are livestock free so your dog will love the freedom. You pass Stanmer House, which is a grade 1 listed mansion, go through the old garden of the mansion and then into beautiful woodland. There is a small section of farmland to cross and then back into wonderful woodland. You will pass a large dewpond where your dog can cool off. Near the end of the walk you will descend across fields where there may be cattle grazing.

How to get there – From the A27 take the A270 turn off, signed for Brighton. Follow the white and brown signs for Stanmer Park. On entering the park, continue on the road, passing many parking bays. Pass Stanmer House, and on reaching a road junction turn right. Follow the sign for the car park, which will be found on your left, opposite the church.

Grid Reference – TQ 337096

Postcode – BN1 9PZ

Parking – Free

Facilities – There are toilets about 200 yards before the car park.

You will need – Dog lead, dog bags.

The Walk

❶ Keep your dog on a lead to begin this walk. From the car park go back onto the access road and turn left. You will pass a pond on your right, and then after the fence, cross the green diagonally left, passing the grand Stanmer House on your far right.

Head for the double iron gates with large brick gateposts to the left of the house. Pass through the gates and pass a private car park on your left. Continue straight ahead and ascend steps into a lawned garden area with an arboretum.

❷ Enter the arboretum and continue straight ahead, then turn right about half way through, where you will see a worn path towards the edge of the garden. Follow the path out of the garden, where you will enter into mixed broadleaved woodland. On your right you will pass some old Victorian gravestones belonging to the pets that lived in the house.

You will pass many greenhouses on your right beyond the walled kitchen garden. Continue on the wide path, and when you reach another path with a field boundary ahead, turn left and then almost immediately right. Continue on this wide path.

On reaching two paths ahead, take the lower path on your right, which is parallel with the field on your right and continue on the woodland edge. The path begins to ascend. A little further on, as you go over a small rise, you will

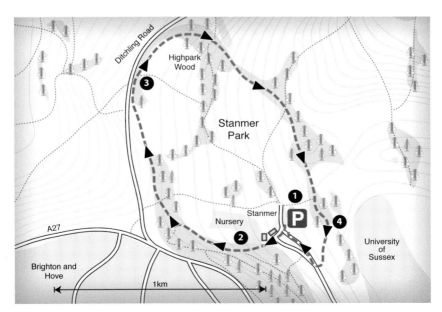

see a gate on your right. Pass this gate and continue beside the field boundary.

The path begins to ascend again and you will pass a number of badger setts, where you will see the excavated chalky soil. Put your dog on a lead here as there is a lane ahead, and for terrier owners it may prevent your dog going underground!

Turn left on the dirt track beside the lane, and when reaching a vehicle barrier on the opposite side of the lane, cross the lane and go through the gap beside the barrier. Continue along the path, straight ahead through the woodland. At the end of the woods you will reach a gate. Pass through the gate, keeping your dog under close control, as there may be livestock. Veer to the left on the worn path heading toward the hedgerow. Follow beside the hedgerow on your right at the edge of the field. Ignore the footpaths on the left and right and continue straight ahead. You will pass a small woodland, which is fenced off from grazing animals, on your right. Continue beside the fence line and at the end there is a pond on your right, where your dog can cool off on a hot day. ❸

Keep the pond on your right and continue straight ahead. Pass through a gate into narrow mixed broadleaved woodland. Keep your dog under close control as there is a road on your left and there isn't a boundary fence to begin with.

Continue on this well-made path. The path will veer away from the road in places. Ignore a path on your left and paths on your left and right, and continue straight ahead. You will pass a metal barn on your far left. The path then leaves the road behind, giving your dog a little more freedom.

You will pass a bridleway marked with a finger post and then cross over a track, continuing straight ahead through the woodland. You will come close to a boundary wall on your left, passing a house beyond the wall. Follow near to this wall, which is dilapidated in places for quite some distance.

The woods narrow again and you will have farmland on both sides. Ignore a path on your right and continue. The path will descend gently. The woodland widens out again and the wall on your left comes to an end. Further along the path you will pass a pylon and cross a track. Shortly after you will reach a fork. Take the path on the right and continue. You will have a field boundary just beyond the trees on your right. The path will soon veer away from the field boundary and there is a beech plantation on your right.

A little further along you will pass a field boundary on your left with wood pasture beyond it. As you continue there is a field boundary on your far right. The woods will expand a little on both sides as you continue. Ignore paths on your left and right and a little further along you will pass a large dew pond on your left. Dogs can cool off here on hot days.

The path descends now and you will reach a gate at the end of the woods. Pass through the gate into a large field. There may be cattle or sheep in the field, therefore keep your dog on a lead or under close control. ❹ Turn right and descend across the field, where you will soon pick up a worn grassy path. Keep to the right of a tree enclosure. You will see Stanmer House ahead and to your right.

Continue on the worn path, passing a holly bush on your right. Head for the trees on the other side of the field. On reaching the field boundary pass through the gate. Turn right on the tarmac road, passing the familiar green on your left. You will soon reach the car park on your right.

14. Ashcombe Bottom
Chall - 6.6 miles - 3hr

This is a fabulous walk, with stunning views and scenery. The walk is partly linear along the South Downs Way, but there is a circular section at the furthest point. You will pass through Ashcombe Bottom woodland, which is mixed broadleaf and has many glades. There is a short, easy ascent through farmland, where gentle cattle graze, and then finishing back along the South Downs Way. Cattle may be grazing throughout the walk, and the paths are also bridleways, therefore you may come across horse riders or cyclists.

How to get there – Ditchling is signposted off the A27, just outside Brighton. Continue on the Ditchling Road, ignoring the first car park on your right (Upper Lodges) until you reach the Ditchling Beacon car park on your left.

Grid Reference – TQ 333129

Parking – Pay by mobile in the Ditchling Beacon car park. National Trust members free.

Facilities – There are no facilities

You will need –Dog leads, dog bags and water for your dog

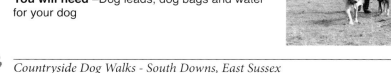

Countryside Dog Walks - South Downs, East Sussex

The Walk

1 Keep your dog on the lead to begin this walk. From the car park entrance, go to the right of the car park and join the long distance footpath, The South Downs Way (SDW), and turn right. You will be met with wonderful views of the surrounding countryside. Descend the steps and cross the road with care. Go through the gate on the opposite side.

Continue on this path, ignoring any footpaths on your left and right, following beside the stock fence on your right. You will be spoilt by the lovely views of the countryside on your left and right, as far as the eye can see. You will pass some hawthorn scrub on your right, and then a little further along there is gorse scrub to your left.

As you continue, the view is lost on your left, but on your right you will see rolling hills and hedgerows, and you will have stock fence on both sides. As you descend a gentle hill you will have wonderful views once again on your left. Continue on, and as you descend another hill you will reach a gate.

Put your dog on a lead or under close control; pass through the gate and cross a track. Continue straight ahead, passing through a gap in the fence to continue on the SDW. Again, ignore any paths on the left and right.

The path ascends with fences on both sides. On reaching another track at a sharp bend, take the right path, which continues with the SDW. This track is used by farm vehicles so take extra care of your dog. Ignore a footpath on

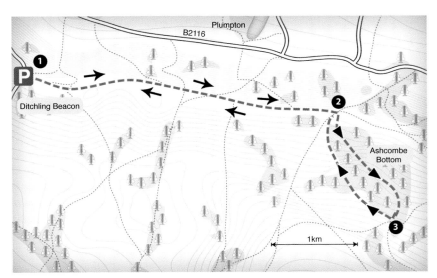

your left and a track on your right. Continue straight ahead. You are now walking along the field edge, as there is no fence on your right.

The path ascends slightly, and you are surrounded by beautiful countryside views. Again ignore any footpaths on your left. On reaching the end of the field, you will be between stock fencing once again. The path descends towards the woodland in the distance.

On reaching a gate ahead, go through it into a field owned by the National Trust known as Black Cap. You have now left the SDW. ❷ Turn right and continue close to the field boundary. You will see a gate ahead. Continue towards the gate, but look ahead and to your left, where you will see another gate as you descend a little. Head for this gate, which takes you into the mixed broadleaved woodland.

The path descends quite steeply to begin with. You will pass several open glades, where the bracken is being managed to make way for wild flowers. You will eventually meet with another track. Continue straight ahead, ignoring the path on your right.

On reaching an open meadow, ignore the path on the left and continue straight ahead. Again, the area is being managed to control bracken. Where the path splits in two, take the narrow path on the left, following the blue way-marker.

A little further on, pass through a gate and continue straight ahead. You now have a field on your right and woodland on your left. At the end of the field, keep your dog under close control and take the gate on your right, which enters into the corner of the field. ❸ Your dog can find water on the right, by way of the drinking trough.

Cross the field diagonally right, ascending on the worn path. You will then reach the right hand side of the field, where you follow alongside the fence line. Look behind at the views, where you can stop and take a rest. When you reach the end of the fence line, keep going straight ahead. You will soon see a gate ahead, as you ascend. Pass through the gate and cross another path; continue straight ahead passing briefly into the shade of the trees.

On reaching a gate go through it and continue straight ahead, crossing a field, heading for the trees, following a slightly rutted grassy track. Pass through the trees and head for the corner of a fence line straight ahead. On reaching the fence line, continue straight ahead on the edge of the field. Pass through a gate and continue straight on.

On meeting another path go through the gate on your left, where you will find yourself back on a familiar path on the SDW. Now continue to retrace your steps, ignoring any paths on your left and right. Remember to put your dog on a lead as you near the car park, before reaching the road.

15. Ditchling Beacon
Med-Chall - 4.5 miles - 2.5hr

This circular walk passes over part of the South Downs Way long distance route. It crosses through beautiful countryside, passing through peaceful farmland, with amazing sloping hills which appear to collide together at the bottom. Stunning views can be seen from parts of the walk. There may be livestock grazing for most of the walk.

How to get there – Ditchling is signposted off the A27, just outside Brighton. Continue on the Ditchling Road, ignoring the first car park on your right (Upper Lodges) until you reach the Ditchling Beacon car park on your left.

Grid Reference – TQ 333129

Parking – Free in the Ditchling Beacon car park

Facilities – There are no facilities

You will need – Dog leads, dog bags and water for your dog

The Walk

1 From the car park, go to the furthest end away from the entrance and enter onto the path, turning left. This is part of the South Downs Way(SDW) long distance path. You will have fantastic views immediately of the countryside and towns, as far as the eye can see. Pass through a gate and continue straight ahead, ascending slightly.

The path soon follows a stock fence on your left and you begin to descend gradually. Pass a footpath on your left and continue straight ahead, with the stock fence and farmland on your left. There are floristic meadows on your right in the summer months. You will stay on the path with views on your right for some distance.

On reaching the end of the stock fence, you will pass through a gate into open farmland. You will now have rolling hills on your far left. A little further along you will pass a dew pond on your left, where your dog can cool off. There is now a stock fence on your right, with gorse scrub. The path will now follow the fence line

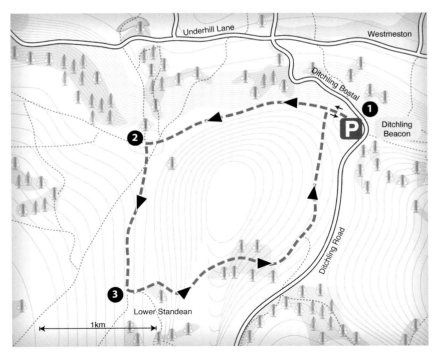

and the gorse scrub. You will pass another dew pond, which is fenced with lovely split-rail oak.

On passing the pond, go through another gate and continue along the worn path. The paths are well defined, with natural flint stone. You will pass through another gate, where you are now between stock fencing. Pass a footpath on your right and then take the footpath on your left, passing through the gate. ❷

Continue following a stock fence on your right, along the edge of an open field, following a bridleway. There may be stock grazing here, or there may be crops growing. There are beautiful rolling hills on your far right. You pass through another gate, where you continue straight ahead, through the middle of a field.

On reaching the end of the field, don't go through the gate but turn left, staying within the field boundary. Follow close to the stock fence on your right, on the well-worn path. Descend to a gate on your right and pass through it. Continue on a farm track. You will pass a red brick barn on your right. Continue on, passing pig sheds, keeping your dog on a lead or under close control as there is electric fencing on your left.

Continue on the track, taking the second path on the left ❸ and then pass through the gate. Follow the stock fence on your right, ascending. Pass through another gate on reaching the end of the field. Now follow the track straight ahead, which cuts across the field. The path will descend and as it gets a little steeper you will be in the valley, where several hills reach level ground. As the path bends to your left you will soon reach a fence line on your right. Follow the fence line in the valley and when reaching a gate in the fence line, pass through it.

Turn left and continue walking along the middle of the field, on a gradual ascent. A path isn't visible to begin with, but it will become more defined as you continue up the hill. Continue walking along the path, through the narrow field. On reaching the end of the field, pass through another gate and then under the mature ash and sycamore trees. You can take a rest here on a hot day, where your dog will enjoy the cool shade. Continue on a gradual ascent, following the grassy path between two hills, which are very floristic in the summer months, with many butterflies and bees.

The gradient steepens as you continue. On meeting another path, turn left and pass through the gate. Now passing between barbed wire fences, still ascending gradually. You will pass through another gate and continue straight ahead, passing the fence line on your left, where you are now on the edge of a field.

Pass through another gate and continue between the barbed wire fence. On leaving the fence line on your right, the area opens up. Continue on the well-worn path, close to the fence on your left. You will again have wonderful views ahead, across miles of countryside and towns. The path descends to meet a gate. Pass through the gate and turn right, where you will find yourself back on a familiar path. Ascend now for a short while, where you will reach back to the car park.

Countryside Dog Walks - South Downs, East Sussex

16. Jack and Jill

Easy - 1.5 miles - 1hr

This is a short circular walk, with wonderful views of the surrounding rolling hills and beautiful countryside. You will see two windmills, which stand side by side, known as Jack and Jill. The walk passes through farm tracks and quiet lanes and along field edges. There may be livestock on parts of this walk.

How to get there – From Brighton leave the A27, following the London, Gatwick turn-off on the A23. Take the first turn-off signed for A273 Hassocks. Ignore the signs for Pyecombe and continue straight ahead. Shortly after passing Three Greys Riding School on your left, take the turning on your right onto Mill Lane. You will soon reach the Jack and Jill car park on your left.

Grid Reference – TQ 302134

Parking – Free in the car park

Facilities – There are no facilities

You will need – Dog lead, dog bags and water for your dog

The Walk

❶ From the car park you can see the two windmills known as Jack and Jill. Jill is the white windmill that has been restored. At the time of writing, Jack had no sails. Continue to the car park entrance and turn left, ascending gently on the farm track.

Ignore a track on your left soon after and continue straight ahead. Ignore a second track on your left. Ignore a blue way-marker and continue straight ahead. On reaching a finger post turn left, **❷** following signs for South Downs Way and Ditchling Beacon. Continue on a gentle ascent. You will have views on your right of the hills and countryside.

Continue between the hedgerows. **❸** Turn right when you reach a path, and continue between stock fencing, with fields on either side. Pass through a gate, keeping your dog under close control or on a lead, and turn right, following beside the stock fence on the edge of the field.

You will have beautiful views straight ahead and on your left across the hilly countryside. At the end of the fence line, pass through a gap beside a gate and turn right on a path, **❹** following the sign for the South Downs Way and Ditchling Beacon. Keep your dog on a lead. Follow the track between the horse paddocks with a post and rail fence and then cross the farmyard. You will pass barns on your right and a farmhouse on your left.

You will see the windmill Jack ahead and to your left. Continue on the farm track. As you pass through a gateway at the end of the farm track ignore another track on your right and continue on a slight descent. Turn right on reaching a blue way-marker. Continue beside a field. As you turn a bend you will gain wonderful views on your right, stretching for miles. You will pass Jack and then Jill on your left. At the end of the path you will reach the car park.

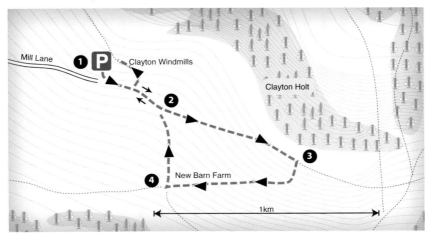

17. Summer Down

Medium - 1.8 miles - 1.5hr

This is a lovely circular walk, crossing meadows with scrub areas. You will have stunning views across the countryside, and as you reach Devil's Dyke the views down the steep-sided valley are impressive. There may be cattle throughout the walk, however, they are a quiet breed accustomed to walkers and dogs. There are a couple of stiles on this walk, but there is a lift gate for dogs. This will be inaccessible for very large breeds of dog.

How to get there – From the A27 take the Hove/Brighton turn-off onto the A2038. Follow the sign for Devil's Dyke at the roundabout. A little further along, ignore the left turn-off signed for Devil's Dyke and continue on the road. Shortly after passing a road on your left you will see the National Trust car park/lay-by on your left.

Grid Reference – TQ 270114
Postcode – BN45 7DB

Parking – Free in the National Trust car park/lay-by

Facilities – There are no facilities

You will need – Dog leads, dog bags

The Walk

❶ From the car park ascend to the gate, go through the pedestrian gate, and then ascend the well-made path on part of the South Downs Way. Ignore the grassy path on your left just after. There is a hedgerow on your right and a meadow on your left with scrub.

As you reach a metal railing fence, you will enter into another meadow with scrub. Continue on the worn path, which veers left through the middle of the meadow. As you ascend there are wonderful views on your right.

You will pass a car park on your left as the path levels out. Continue on the path, which will become obvious again after passing the car park. Pass through some scrub and a little further along, on reaching an opening as you turn a bend, the views will be seen once more. Ignore the gate over on your left.

You will pass a water trough on your right for if your dog needs a drink. You will pass through scrub once again and then through a pedestrian gate. **❷** There are now two options, A. The short route or B. The longer route which adds another fifteen minutes to your walk.

A. Turn immediately right, leaving the path, and follow the   edge of the hawthorn scrub. You will soon see another small path, which descends towards a finger post. On reaching another path turn right, heading down into the steep-sided valley known as Devil's Dyke. The views are fabulous here, across the valley to the hills beyond.

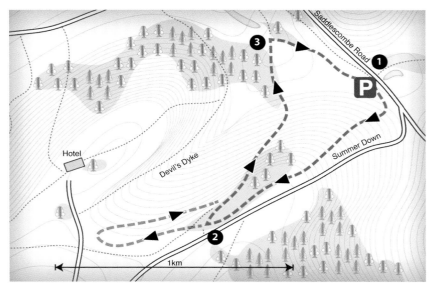

B. Continue straight ahead on the well-made path. The scrub will clear again to provide views on your right. Continue on the path until you reach a gate. Don't go through the gate but turn right. The path will be unclear now but continue near to the field boundary and descend the hill. You will see Devil's Dyke (the valley) on your right.

Head towards the gate and the path below, but take the first well-defined path on your right, staying on this side of Devil's Dyke. Continue on the path ascending with stunning views looking down into Devil's Dyke on your left. The path becomes a little unclear as you go through the scrub. Continue in the direction you have been going and you will pick it up again as you continue. You will either see the path which descends to a finger post, which you should take, or you will return to the gate at option A. If you have returned to the gate follow the directions for option A.

Both routes re-join here. Continue on this path, descending into the valley. The path bends sharply to the left as you continue. You will reach a small gate. Pass through the gate and descend gently beneath the trees. After about fifty yards you will reach a yellow way-marker. ❸ Turn right here onto a narrow path, and ascend to a stile. There is a lift gate for dogs. Cross the stile, keeping your dog under close control or on a lead as there may be livestock grazing. Continue straight ahead on a wider path. On reaching the opening into a hilly field turn left.

Stay close to the field edge and continue. On reaching a tarmac path turn right. Put your dog on a lead as there is a busy road ahead. Ascend on the path and soon you will reach a farm gate. Cross the stile on the right of the gate. On reaching the road turn right and you will soon reach the car park ahead.

18. Devil's Dyke

Medium - 1.2 miles - 1.5hr

This is a beautiful circular walk passing the side of the Devil's Dyke, which was formed by the last ice age. It is the longest, deepest dry valley in Britain and a super sight to see. You will then continue to descend steeply through beautiful woodland. There are fabulous views of the surrounding countryside. There may be cattle grazing for a section of this walk.

How to get there – From the A27 take the Hove/Brighton turn-off onto the A 2038. Follow the sign for Devil's Dyke. Turn onto a minor road, following the sign for Devil's Dyke, and after passing a car park on your right continue and take the next turn-off on your left, where you will soon reach the car park.

Grid Reference – TQ 258110
Postcode – BN1 8YJ

Parking - Pay and Display, National Trust

Facilities – There are no facilities

You will need – Dog lead, dog bags and water for your dog

The Walk

1 Start this walk near to the bus turning area, at the entrance to the car park. With your back to the Devil's Dyke Pub, take the footpath straight ahead. Descend on the gravel path, with stunning views on your left.

Take the second path on your left, before reaching a gate ahead. Follow the grassy path, with a clear view of Devil's Dyke on your right. The path cuts through a meadow, which is lovely in the summer months, with many flowers attracting butterflies and bees.

Pass through a gate and continue straight ahead, ignoring the path on your left. You will have scrub on your right now and as you descend a little the views will open up straight ahead.

Ignore another path on your left, and the path will now descend quite steeply. You will head towards mixed broadleaved woodland. Pass through another gate on reaching the woods. **2** The path continues to descend. Look out for a path on your left, with steps. **3** Ascend the steps and follow the worn, narrow path through the trees.

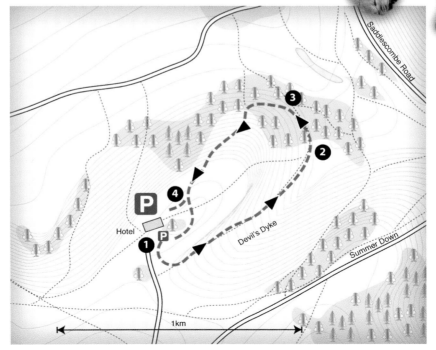

80

Just after reaching a stock fence, pass through a kissing gate and ascend the steps through hazel coppiced woodland. As you leave the woodland, the views on your right are fabulous, with rolling hills and then countryside for miles. Continue your ascent, but don't forget to stop, catch your breath and have a look behind you at the impressive views.

Continue on, where the path will level for a short spell along the cutting of the hillside. Stay on this path, which will ascend once again. As the path bends to the right, you will have wonderful views on your right. On reaching a stock fence, pass through the kissing gate and take the middle path. Cross a path almost immediately and then take the path on the right.

You will see a telescope ahead and the car park on your left.

19. Three Hill Tops

Medium - 3.5 miles - 1.5hr

This walk is linear with a loop at the furthest end. There is beautiful scenery throughout the walk, with views across a hilly landscape to beautiful isolated villages. There are new views as you climb each hill top. You will pass an Iron Age hill fort. The three hill tops have gradual ascents and require little effort. The walk is predominantly across farmland so you will need to keep your dog under close control. There are no roads on this walk, but there are a couple of stiles, with lift gates for your dog.

How to get there – From the A27 take the Hove/Brighton turn-off onto the A 2038. Follow the sign for Devil's Dyke. Turn onto a minor road, following the sign for Devil's Dyke. After passing a car park on your right, continue and take the next turn-off on your left, where you will soon reach the car park.

Grid Reference – TQ 258110
Postcode – BN1 8YJ

Parking - Pay and Display, National Trust

Facilities – There are no facilities

You will need – Dog lead, dog bags and water for your dog

Countryside Dog Walks - South Downs, East Sussex

The Walk

1 Start at the front of the Devil's Dyke Pub, cross the entrance road and then cross the grass bank. Pass through the kissing gate and follow the South Downs Way long distance path. You will have amazing views to your right, with countryside for as far as you can see.

Pass a ruined brick building on your left and continue on the undulating path, across the top of the beautiful sloping hills. There are many wild flowers in the summer months, and the sides of the hills have many wrinkles which look similar to the shape of the sand after the tide has gone out.

2 Take the path on your right, just before reaching the fence line ahead. Pass through a gate and take the left path at the fork, on a slight ascent. There may be cattle grazing, but this is a very popular path so the cattle shouldn't bother you. Please keep your dog under close control whilst amongst livestock.

Follow the worn grassy path, with views on your right over Folking village and beyond. You will pass close to the windswept hawthorn scrub and if you look to your left you will glimpse the sea. The path widens, you pass through a gate, and then you ascend for a short spell.

Take the grassy path on your right and a little further on you will pass a pylon. Cross a track and ascend the small bank, where you meet a stile. Do not go over the stile, but turn right **3** and follow beside the fence line. On reaching another stile on your left, cross over it and use the lift gate for your dog.

Continue straight ahead, following beside the stock fence on your left. The

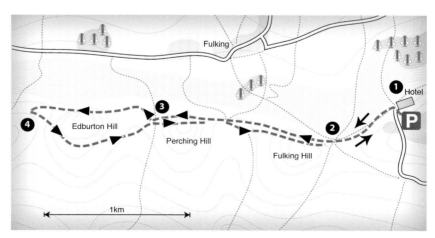

path ascends on the edge of the hillside. You will pass a row of trees on your left and then cross over another stile, which has a gap for your dog.

Cross the field diagonally to your right, following the worn path, crossing through the middle of an Iron Age hill fort. You will clearly see the motte and bailey. You will soon follow alongside a fence line on your left, descending for some distance. Follow the fence line around a sharp left bend. Shortly afterwards pass through a gate and turn left on a track, passing through another gate to re-join the South Downs Way. **4**

Follow the track to the right of the field, beside the stock fence, ascending to begin with. Ignore a stile on your right as the path begins to descend. The views open up with sea views on your right.

You will reach a junction with gates. Go straight ahead, passing through the gate, and follow the path beside the fence line. On your far left, you will pass a familiar pylon. Ascend on the path, quite steeply to begin with, with views on your left once again. As you reach the top of the hill, you can see a familiar route ahead.

Pass through the gate and retrace your steps. On passing through the gate ahead, remember to take the path which veers to the left, heading back towards the pub in the distance and back to the car park.

20. Beeding Hill

Medium - 3.3 miles - 1.5hr

You will have splendid views throughout this walk and the landscape stretches for miles, with rolling hill scenes, and some sea views. You will feel that you are miles from anywhere, whilst walking amongst farmland. There may be sheep grazing for parts of this walk, but a lot of the paths are fenced on both sides of the footpath, separating you and your dog from livestock. There is a quiet road, which is part of the South Downs Way long distance trail.

How to get there – From Brighton take the A27 signed for Portsmouth and Horsham. Take the turning signed for Horsham, Shoreham and Steyning on the A283. At the roundabout turn left, following signs for Shoreham. At the next roundabout turn left onto Upper Shoreham road. Turn left onto Erringham Road, following the brown signs for Mill Hill and Youth Hostel. Continue to follow the brown signs, passing Mill Hill Local Nature Reserve on your left. After some distance you will reach the car park on your left at a sharp bend in the road.

Grid Reference – TQ 208096   **Nearest Postcode** – BN43 5FB

Parking – Free in the car park

Facilities – There are no facilities

You will need – Dog lead, dog bags and water for your dog

Countryside Dog Walks - South Downs, East Sussex

The Walk

❶ From the car park go onto the road, and turn left and then immediately right to pass through a gate, keeping your dog on a lead or under close control as there may be sheep grazing. Turn left and ascend gently on the worn path beside the stock fence at the edge of a field. You will have instant views if you look behind you. You can see sea views and a small airport on your right.

Pass some hawthorn trees and the countryside then opens up, with vast open space across the large agricultural fields. Pass through a gate into another large field and continue to follow the stock fence on the edge of the field. The path levels off for some distance and then begins to descend.

Pass through another gate and continue between stock fences with fields on each side. Your dog can be let off the lead, as long as you are sure he won't jump the fences. Keep him under close control just in case the fences are in poor condition to ensure he doesn't get into the fields.

Truleigh Hill

3

Freshcombe and
Summersdeane
Farm

Mill Hill

Bushy Bottom

P

Beeding Hill

1

Mill Hill

2

1km

As you descend you can see the wonderful rolling hills that are so typical of the South Downs. You will reach a dip and then ascend, where the path will now get a little stony and rocky. As you pass between old gateposts the gradient will lessen a little. You will pass an open storage area on your left and then you will reach another wider track.

❷ Turn left on the track between two fields, again with a stock fence on each side. Continue on the track, heading for the houses in the distance. Keep your dog on a lead as you pass the houses and farm buildings.

You will reach another track after passing the buildings and a horse paddock on your left. Turn left on this track and descend. ❸ Pass the horse paddock on your left. A little further on you will pass a youth hostel on your right. You will then pass a row of Scots pine on both sides of the track.

You will reach a tarmac road, where you will be met with endless views in all directions. Continue on this road on a gentle descent for about a quarter of a mile, where you will reach the car park on your right.

Countryside Dog Walks - South Downs, East Sussex

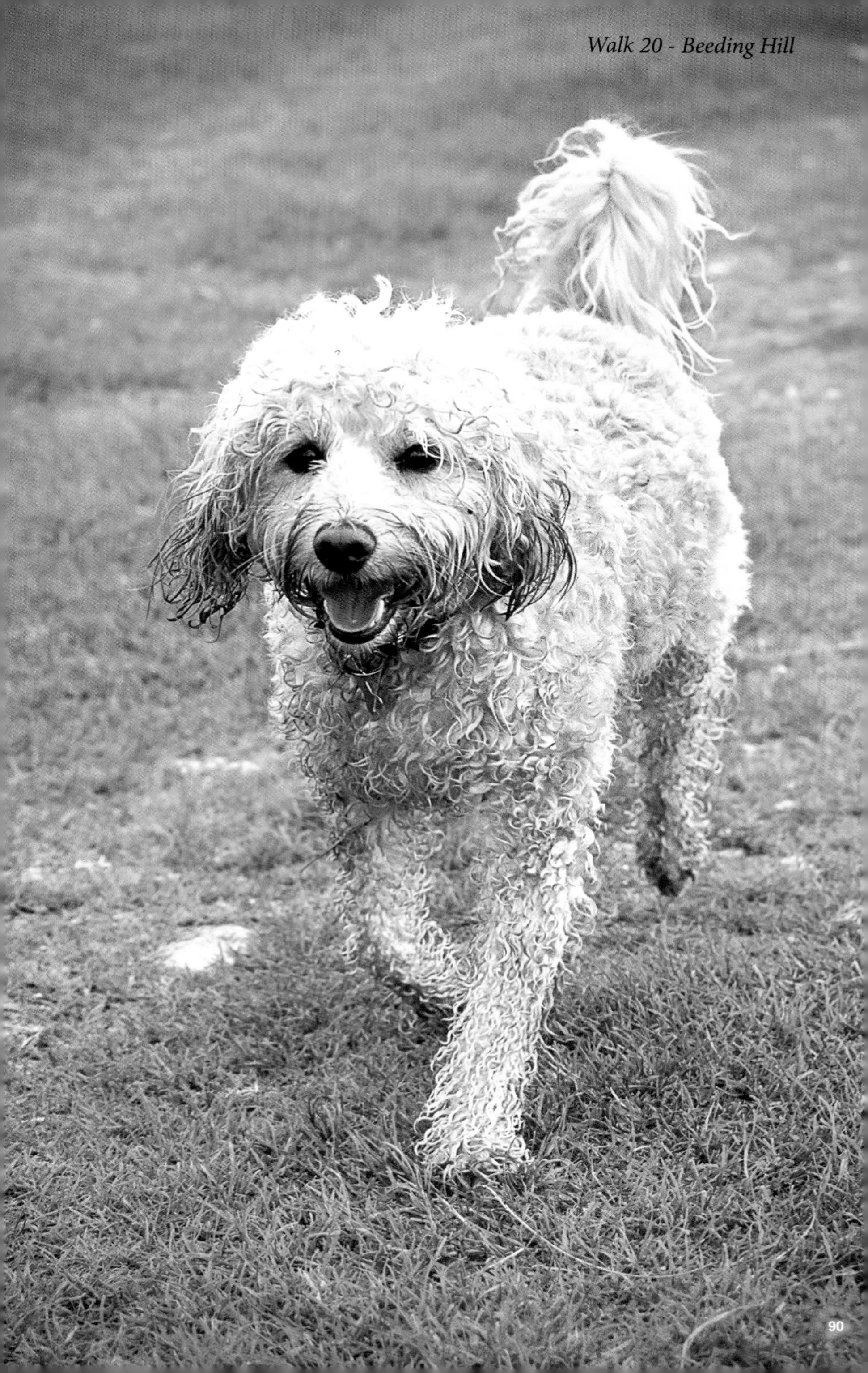

www.countrysidedogwalks.co.uk

Countryside Dog Walks & Dog Friendly Pub Walks

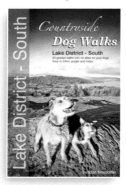

Lake District - South

Countryside Dog Walks
Lake District - South
20 graded walks with no stiles for your dogs
Easy to follow guides and maps

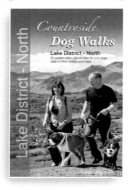

Lake District - North

Countryside Dog Walks
Lake District - North
20 graded walks with no stiles for your dogs
Easy to follow guides and maps

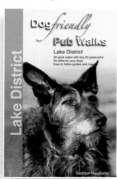

Lake District

Dog friendly Pub Walks
Lake District
20 great walks with dog 96 great pubs
No stiles for your dogs
Easy to follow guides and maps

Peak District - North

Countryside Dog Walks
Peak District - North
Dark Peak Area
20 graded walks with no stiles for your dogs
Easy to follow guides and maps

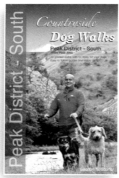

Peak District - South

Countryside Dog Walks
Peak District - South
White Peak Area
20 graded walks with no stiles for your dogs
Easy to follow guides and maps

Snowdonia

Countryside Dog Walks
Snowdonia
20 graded walks with no stiles for your dogs
Easy to follow guides and maps

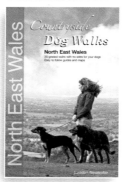

North East Wales

Countryside Dog Walks
North East Wales
20 graded walks with no stiles for your dogs
Easy to follow guides and maps

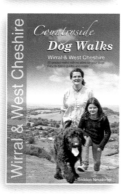

Wirral & West Cheshire

Countryside Dog Walks
Wirral & West Cheshire
20 graded walks with no stiles for your dogs
Easy to follow guides and maps

Follow us on Facebook for progress reports on our future publications.

Search - Countryside Dog Walks

Wet Nose Publishing Ltd